I0413253

science for a changing world

Prepared in cooperation with the U.S. Fish and Wildlife Service

A Comparison of Mercury Burdens between St. Marks National Wildlife Refuge and St. Andrew Bay, Florida: Evaluation of Fish Body Burdens and Physiological Responses in Largemouth Bass, Spotted Seatrout, Striped Mullet, and Sunfish

By D.H. Huge, R.H. Rauschenberger, C.M. Wieser, and J.M. Hemming

Open-File Report 2011–1056

U.S. Department of the Interior
U.S. Geological Survey

U.S. Department of the Interior
KEN SALAZAR, Secretary

U.S. Geological Survey
Marcia K. McNutt, Director

U.S. Geological Survey, Reston, Virginia 2011

For product and ordering information:
World Wide Web: http://www.usgs.gov/pubprod
Telephone: 1-888-ASK-USGS

For more information on the USGS—the Federal source for science about the Earth,
its natural and living resources, natural hazards, and the environment:
World Wide Web: http://www.usgs.gov
Telephone: 1-888-ASK-USGS

Suggested citation:
Huge, D.H., Rauschenberger, R.H., Wieser, C.M., and Hemming, J.M., 2011, A comparison of mercury
burdens between St. Marks National Wildlife Refuge and St. Andrew Bay, Florida: Evaluation of fish body
burdens and physiological responses in largemouth bass, spotted seatrout, striped mullet, and sunfish: U.S.
Geological Survey Open-File Report 2011-1056, 35 p.

Contents

Figures

Tables

Conversion Factors

Multiply	By	To obtain
micrometer (μm)	0.0003937	inch (in.)
millimeter (mm)	0.03937	inch (in.)
meter (m)	3.1	foot (ft)
kilometer (km)	0.6214	mile (mi)
milligrams per kilogram (mg/kg)	1	parts per million (ppm)
nanograms per gram (ng/g)	1	parts per billion (ppb)

Acronyms

GSI	Gonadosomatic Index
GSMFC	Gulf States Marine Fisheries Commission
Hg	Mercury
$HgC_4H_6O_4C$	Mercuric II acetate
Hg_2Cl_2	Mercurous I chloride
$HgCH_3$	Methyl mercury
HSI	Hepatosomatic Index
mg	Milligram
ng	Nanogram
NWR	National Wildlife Refuge
ppb	Parts per billion
ppm	Parts per million
μg	Microgram
USEPA	United States Environmental Protection Agency
USGS-SESC	United States Geological Survey-Southeast Ecological Science Center

A Comparison of Mercury Burdens between St. Marks National Wildlife Refuge and St. Andrew Bay, Florida: Evaluation of Fish Body Burdens and Physiological Responses in Largemouth Bass, Spotted Seatrout, Striped Mullet, and Sunfish

By D.H. Huge[1], R.H. Rauschenberger[2], C.M. Wieser[1], and J.M. Hemming[3]

Abstract

Musculature from the dorsal region of 130 largemouth bass (*Micropterus salmoides*), 140 sunfish (*Lepomis* sp.), 41 spotted seatrout (*Cynoscion nebulosus*) and 67 striped mullet (*Mugil cephalus*) were collected from five estuarine and five freshwater sites within the St. Marks National Wildlife Refuge and two estuarine and two freshwater sites from St. Andrew Bay, Florida, United States of America. Musculature was analyzed for total mercury content, sagittal otoliths were removed for age determination and physiological responses were measured. Largemouth bass and sunfish from the refuge had higher mercury concentrations in musculature than those from the bay. Male spotted seatrout, male striped mullet, male and female sunfish and female largemouth bass had mercury burdens positively correlated with length. The majority of all four species of fish from both study areas contained mercury levels below 1.5 part per million, the limit for safe consumption recommended the Florida Department of Health. In comparison, a significant percentage of largemouth bass and sunfish from several sampled sites, most notably Otter Lake and Lake Renfroe within St. Marks National Wildlife Refuge, had mercury levels consistent with the health department's guidelines of "limited consumption" or "no consumption guidelines."

Introduction

Although mercury is a universal contaminant in the biosphere, its distribution is not uniform (U.S. Environmental Protection Agency [USEPA], 2001b; Gulf States Marine Fisheries Commission, 2002). Mercury sources can be natural or anthropogenic. Natural mercury sources include volcanoes and geothermal activity, forest fires, degassing of sediment or rock containing mercury, and seawater evaporation. The majority of anthropogenic sources of mercury include combustion processes where mercury is emitted as a byproduct, mining practices, sewage discharge, and metal refining operations (U.S. Environmental Protection Agency, 2006).

---

[1] D.H. Huge (*dane_huge@usgs.gov*; 352-264-3540) and C. M. Wieser, U.S. Geological Survey-Southeast Ecological Science Center, 7920 NW 71st Street, Gainesville, Florida 32653.
[2] R. H. Rauschenberger, U.S. Fish and Wildlife Service, 6620 Southpoint Drive South, Suite 310, Jacksonville, Florida 32216.
[3] J. M. Hemming, U.S. Fish and Wildlife Service, 1601 Balboa Avenue, Panama City, Florida 32405.

Understanding mercury distribution, or the fate and transport of mercury contamination, is paramount to protecting fish and wildlife species, as well as the human population. (Florida Department of Environmental Protection, 2007).

The distribution of mercury depends on local and global source locations, air currents, physiochemical properties of the receiving environments, biotic and abiotic transformations, and biomagnification in certain animal species (Suter, 1993; Beyer and others, 1997). Much of the world's mercury contamination travels in global air currents until eventual deposition onto land surface. Mercury enters aquatic environments through runoff of land deposits or direct deposition into water bodies. Mercury is biologically transformed to methyl mercury ($HgCH_3$) in the aquatic environment. $HgCH_3$ has an inherent tendency to concentrate in biological organisms, particularly aquatic species, through incremental increases during transfer from the water to phytoplankton to zooplankton to planktivorous (plankton eating) fish to piscivorous fish, birds, wildlife, and humans (U.S. Environmental Protection Agency, 2001a).

Numerous reports have documented that $HgCH_3$ is more toxic to fish and wildlife than inorganic forms, such as mercuric II acetate ($HgC_4H_6O_4C$) and mercurous I chloride (Hg_2Cl_2). These reports include behavioral effects and reproductive impairment resulting from neurological damage caused by $HgCH_3$ exposure in fish and wildlife (Scherer, 1975; Scheuhammer, 1991; Suter, 1993; Clarkson, 1994; Beyer and others, 1997). These effects also extend to humans, particularly during prenatal exposure (D'Itri and D'Itri, 1977; U.S. Environmental Protection Agency, 2001a; Gulf States Marine Fisheries Commission, 2002).

The ten states within the U.S. Fish and Wildlife Service Southeast Region have issued fish consumption advisories due to mercury contamination (Facemire and others, 1995). More recently, Florida and the other Gulf Coast states have issued statewide mercury-based consumption advisories on select fish species (U.S. Environmental Protection Agency, 2001a). Additionally, reports of mercury-contaminated fish in northwest Florida are of particular regional concern due to relatively high seafood consumption in the area and seafood's importance to the local economy through fish export and tourism (Brim and others, 1992, 1994; Rider and Adams, 2000). The problematic effects of elevated mercury levels on wildlife are well documented (Royals and Lange, 1990; Facemire and Chlebowski, 1991; Wood and others, 1993; Adams and others, 1998), including migratory birds, marine mammals, and other aquatic and semi-aquatic species (Stickney and others, 1975; Heinz, 1979; Gulf States Marine Fisheries Commission, 2002).

Concerns over potential health risks from the consumption of mercury-contaminated Gulf of Mexico fish instigated the development of a Gulf-wide initiative to examine the extent of mercury contamination in fish (Gulf States Marine Fisheries Commission 2002). The number of mercury-contaminated fish advisories has increased consistently in the United States over recent years (U.S. Environmental Protection Agency, 2001b). Gulf-states fish consumption advisories are common (up to 100 advisories per year) and often statewide due to unacceptable high levels of mercury found in fish that inhabit various aquatic ecosystems (U.S. Environmental Protection Agency, 2001b). The level of mercury recommended for human fish consumption in Florida is based on the action level of 1.0 part per million (ppm; mg/kg ww), as set by the U.S. Food and Drug Administration and World Health Organization. This recommendation is as follows: unlimited consumption of fish when mercury concentrations are under 0.5 ppm, limited consumption of fish when concentrations are between 0.5 and 1.5 ppm (young children and women of childbearing age are most at risk), and no fish consumption when concentrations exceed 1.5 ppm.

Problems exist with national and global mercury criteria. For example, the level at which mercury is known to be detrimental to the developing child is highly uncertain and under much debate (Clapp and Grandjean, 2002). Some studies report that negative effect levels are far lower than action levels currently used to warn people of possible dangers (Clapp and Grandjean, 2002). The action levels of mercury for fish and wildlife are even more uncertain. Additionally, it is not rare for midsized piscivorous fish to contain mercury concentrations that exceed limited consumption thresholds (Brim and others, 1992, 1994; Rider and Adams, 2000). These fish may serve as sentinels or biological indicators of the level of mercury contamination in piscivorous birds and other fish-eating organisms. Certain mercury levels measured in these fish have been reported to cause behavioral and reproductive problems in fish-eating birds and other piscivorous wildlife species (Stickney and others, 1975, Heinz, 1979, Royals and Lange, 1990, Facemire and Chlebowski 1991, Wood and others, 1993, Adams and others, 1998). However, relatively small sample sizes within selected species have been examined to determine levels of mercury contamination due to the large areas that need to be evaluated. A firm understanding of the relative state of mercury levels in unique ecosystems, such as wildlife refuges, would provide important information for policy development and decision making involving fishery status, management actions, and the need for land acquisition to provide buffers between source inputs and sensitive resources.

National wildlife refuges provide sanctuaries for fish and wildlife resources including federally listed endangered and threatened species, migratory birds, and anadromous fish species. Fish and wildlife species living on wildlife refuges, however, are subject to mercury exposure. Changes in land use can alter the natural environment, resulting in greater than normal concentrations of mercury uptake, which progresses upward through the food chain. The main objective of this study was to conduct a comparative assessment of mercury contamination and fish health indicators for several species of fish from St. Marks National Wildlife Refuge (NWR) and St. Andrew Bay, and to compare these results to State of Florida Fish Consumption Advisories.

Acknowledgments

Funding for this project was provided by the U.S. Fish and Wildlife Service and the U.S. Geological Survey. Numerous people played critical roles in the completion of this project. In particular we thank Lynn Lefebvre, Robert Dorazio, and Tim Bargar for their assistance and/or peer review; Travis Smith and Robert Lewis for their assistance in field work and sample collection; Joe Reinman and Michael Keys for their logistical support at St. Marks National Wildlife Refuge; and others who substantially helped in the review and preparation of this report.

Objectives and Hypotheses (H_0)

- Evaluate mercury levels in fish musculature from largemouth bass (*Micropterus salmoides*), spotted seatrout (*Cynoscion nebulosus*), striped mullet (*Mugil cephalus*), and sunfish (*Lepomis* sp.), and conduct area-specific comparisons among species from various trophic levels and/or feeding strategies. Compare sample sites within the St. Marks NWR and St. Andrew Bay (non-national wildlife refuge area). Compare with other mercury data from previous studies along the Gulf Coast.
  - Hypothesis: There is no difference between mercury concentrations in fish musculature taken within areas of St. Marks NWR or St. Andrew Bay.

- Compare biomarkers of fish health between fish collected at St. Marks NWR and those sampled at St. Andrew Bay.
  - Hypothesis: Biomarkers of fish health are not different between fish collected at St. Marks NWR and fish sampled at St. Andrews Bay (non-national wildlife refuge area).
- Assess the general and reproductive health of largemouth bass, spotted seatrout, striped mullet, and sunfish with respect to relative mercury contamination. Assessments will include use of total mercury concentrations in fish musculature, gonadosomatic index (GSI), and hepatosomatic index (HSI).
  - Hypothesis: mercury fish tissue concentration will not be significantly correlated with GSI and HSI.
- Assess species-specific size and age relative to mercury levels in musculature. Data will be examined to determine relationships between fish size, age, and mercury contamination for potential use in developing slot limits or consumptive restrictions based on size.
  - Hypothesis: There is no relationship between fish size and the amount of mercury in fish musculature.
  - Hypothesis: There is no relationship between the age of sampled fish and the amount of mercury found in the musculature.
- Assess the percentage of sampled fish that exceeded State of Florida Fish Consumption Advisories.

The results of these objectives will provide information that benefits local resource managers. For example, knowledge of the state of contamination within and around St. Marks NWR may help resource managers develop management and policy strategies for specific areas that benefit fish and wildlife and mitigate potential risks. Furthermore, finding higher mercury concentrations in fish from St. Andrew Bay (non-national wildlife refuge area) may indicate differences in local mercury inputs and underscore the value of St. Marks NWR and the National Wildlife Refuge System. Lastly, given the increasing industrial and residential development occurring in the Florida Panhandle, resource managers need data on pre-urbanization contaminant loading to better protect trust resources now and in the future.

Methods

Sampling Locations and Fish Collection

Mullet and seatrout were collected from estuarine sites, and sunfish and largemouth bass were collected from freshwater sites within St. Marks NWR (fig. 1) and the St. Andrew Bay watershed (fig. 2). A total of 358 adult fish were collected for total mercury analysis. A total of 243 fish were collected from St. Marks NWR; 73 from five sites within estuarine ecosystems and 170 from five sites within freshwater ecosystems. For the St. Andrew Bay watershed, a total of 10 spotted seatrout were caught from two estuarine sites. A composite site sample of 25 striped mullet was purchased from a local commercial fishing supplier (Miller & Ellis Seafood, Panama City, Florida) who had caught the fish in St. Andrew Bay within the past 24 hours. Largemouth bass (n = 40) and sunfish (n = 40) were collected from two freshwater sites. Twenty fish were collected to provide sufficient statistical analysis power, given the variability reported in previous evaluations of mercury contamination of this national wildlife refuge and elsewhere along the Gulf.

All freshwater fish and striped mullet, with the exception of the purchased mullet, were collected with a boat-mounted Smith-Root GPP-9.0 Electrofisher (Vancouver, Washington, USA). Spotted seatrout were collected using traditional rod and reel fishing techniques, using artificial lures as bait. All fish were processed within 24 hours of their collection.

Fish processing was performed according to standard operating procedures (Environmental Protection Agency, 2000) to minimize risk of cross contamination. Generally, measurements were taken upon collection and included length, weight, gonad weight, liver weight, and sex. Sagittal otoliths were collected in the field as fish were processed for inclusion of age as a determinant parameter (Nielson and Johnson, 1983). Spotted seatrout and mullet otoliths were processed and mounted by the Florida Fish and Wildlife Conservation Commission Fish and Wildlife Research Institute, St. Petersburg, Florida, and age was determined by U.S. Geological Survey-Florida Integrated Science Center (USGS-SESC), Gainesville, Florida (Nielson and Johnson, 1983, Vanderkooy and Guindon-Tisdel, 2003). Largemouth bass and sunfish otoliths were processed and read by the South Carolina Cooperative Fish and Wildlife Research Unit, Clemson, South Carolina. A muscle tissue sample (fillet without the skin) was taken from the dorsal region, posterior to the first dorsal fin, wrapped in aluminum foil, and placed in a plastic bag on wet ice. Three filet knives were rotated throughout collections. Prior to collecting each sample, individual knives were first rinsed in soapy water, tap water, ethyl-alcohol, and finally acetone to remove possible organics. Upon returning to the laboratory, samples were frozen at -20°C until mercury analysis was performed.

Mercury Analyses

Total mercury analyses were performed by the USGS-SESC Ecotoxicology Laboratory. Fish musculature samples were analyzed by using a direct mercury analyzer (Milestone DMA-80), and processed using the following USEPA (1998) method:

> Controlled heating in an oxygenated decomposition furnace was used to liberate from solid and aqueous samples in the instrument. The sample was dried and then thermally and chemically decomposed within the decomposition furnace. The decomposition products are carried by flowing oxygen to the catalytic section of the furnace. Here, oxidation is completed and halogens and nitrogen/sulfur oxides are trapped. The remaining decomposition products were then carried to an amalgamator that selectively traps mercury. After the system is flushed with oxygen to remove any remaining gases or decomposition products, the amalgamator is rapidly heated, releasing mercury vapor. Flowing oxygen carries the vapor through absorbance cells positioned in the light path of a single wavelength atomic absorption spectrophotometer. Absorbance (peak height or peak area) is measured at 253.7 nm as a function of mercury concentration.

The typical working range for this method is 0.05–600 ng and the instrument detection limit for this method is 0.01 ng total mercury. This method is accepted for the Resource Conservation Recovery Act work as method 7473.

Statistical Analyses

With respect to sample location and sex, descriptive statistics were calculated for length (mm), weight (g), age (yr), mercury tissue concentrations (ng/g ww), HSI (liver weight/BW), and GSI (gonad weight/BW) for each species. Prior to comparison, size characteristics, mercury concentrations, and biomarkers were evaluated and met necessary assumptions for parametric tests (normality and homogeneity of variance). Comparisons of endpoints between St. Andrew Bay and St. Marks NWR (Ho #1, #2) were conducted using a mixed model procedure appropriate for nested, unbalanced designs (SAS/STAT software PROC MIXED, Version 9.1.3, SAS Institute, 2000-2004) to determine if differences existed among size parameters, mercury tissue concentrations, and health indicators. Samples of individual fish were nested within each respective area. Comparisons of size parameters, tissue concentrations, HSI, and GSI were conducted separately for each species and gender because of the ecological and physiological differences between species and genders. For example, endpoints in male bass from St. Andrew Bay were compared to those of male bass from St. Marks NWR. Data are presented as mean ± SE, unless otherwise noted.

Associations among biomarkers were examined with Pearson correlation coefficients to determine interactions between tissue mercury concentrations and size and age (Ho #3) (SAS/STAT software PROC CORR, Version 9.1.3, SAS Institute, 2000-2004). Pearson correlation coefficients were also calculated between mercury tissue concentrations and size and age parameters for each species, with genders, sample sites, and areas combined (Ho #4). The reason for examining each species by combining gender, sample sites, and areas for each species was that species-specific length limits are likely the most practical way to manage and set guidelines for fish harvest. For example, if length and mercury tissue concentrations were positively correlated in bass and indicated that bass larger than 12 inches in length are not safe for human consumption, then management guidelines or regulations could be developed that advise or require people to release bass above 12 inches in length.

Correlations among mercury tissue concentrations, HSI, and GSI were conducted to evaluate relationships between health or reproductive endpoints and mercury exposure, because mercury is a neurotoxin (Goyer and Clarkson, 2001) and endocrine disruptor (Gross and others, 2003). Correlations were conducted for each species and gender to control for the species and gender-specific differences that may affect HSI and GSI.

For each sampling site and species, the percentage of sampled fish that exceeded State of Florida Fish Consumption Advisories was calculated as the number of fish with mercury tissue concentrations exceeding advisories divided by the total number of fish collected (specific aim #5). This analysis aids in identifying the extent of mercury contamination within a population within a site and the relative extent of contamination in populations among sites.

Results

Mean length, weight, age, mercury concentration, HSI, and GSI were determined by study area (refuge and non-refuge), sampling site, and sex of each species of fish collected (tables 1-4). The highest mean mercury concentration in fish musculature samples (1.234 ± 0.481 ppm; table 5) was found in largemouth bass from Lake Renfroe (fig. 1) at the St. Marks NWR, and the lowest (0.003 ± 0.002 ppm) was found in striped mullet from the Lower Wakulla River (part of the refuge). The highest individual mercury concentration (2.412 ppm) was detected in a single largemouth bass sample from the St. Marks NWR, and the lowest (0.001 ppm) was detected in a single striped mullet sample, also from the refuge.

Results support the hypothesis that overall differences in mercury tissue concentrations exist among largemouth bass, spotted seatrout, sunfish, and striped mullet (fig. 3). Further, the two freshwater species, largemouth bass and sunfish, sampled from the refuge had significantly higher mercury concentrations ($p = 0.00002$ and $p = 3.06 \times 10^{-8}$, respectively) than those from the bay (fig. 4). The mercury concentration values in the freshwater species from the refuge were notably higher than those from the bay (χ = 859 vs. 528 ppb for St. Marks and St. Andrew bass, respectively, and χ = 366 and 130 ppb for St. Marks vs. St. Andrew sunfish, respectively; fig.4, table 5). Mercury concentration in sunfish from the Deer Point collection site in St. Andrew Bay was an order of magnitude higher than the Martin Bay site (232 vs. 28 ppb). The relatively low concentration (91ppb) in sunfish from the Upper Wakulla River in St. Marks NWR was also noteworthy (figs. 1 and 2; table 5).

Conversely, the estuarine species, striped mullet and spotted seatrout, taken from St. Andrew Bay had significantly higher mercury concentrations (p = 0.00008 and 0.01520, respectively, than those from St. Marks NWR (fig. 4). However, the differences in mercury concentration values in the estuarine species from these two collection areas were not as striking as the differences between the freshwater species (fig. 4; tables 5-7).

Correlations among mercury tissue burdens and fish length, weight, age, HSI, and GSI were evaluated by area, species and sex to determine the relationships among mercury burdens, physical characteristics, and health and reproductive function (tables 6-9). In male and female striped mullet, mercury burdens were positively correlated with GSI (table 8), and mean GSI was greater in male specimens from St. Andrew Bay (3.14) than St. Marks NWR (0.09) (table 7). Female sunfish had a negative correlation between mercury and gonadosomatic index (table 9), and similar mean GSI values for specimens from St. Andrew Bay and St. Marks NWR (table 6). No clear pattern of correlation emerged for any other species between mercury and HSI or GSI (tables 8-9).

Length and weight were highly correlated for both female and male largemouth bass (r= 0.96 and 0.92, respectively), female and male sunfish (r=0.93 and 0.92 respectively), and spotted seatrout females (r=0.96) (tables 8-9). Age was significantly correlated with mercury concentration for all species but mullet (tables 8-11). Age was correlated with length and weight for all species (tables 10-11).

To examine the potential for using size limits as a risk guidance tool, the relationships between mercury burdens, length, and age were evaluated for each species (tables 10-11). For largemouth bass, mercury burdens were correlated with age > weight > length, respectively. For sunfish, mercury burdens were correlated with age > length > weight, respectively. For spotted seatrout, mercury burdens were correlated with age > weight > length, respectively. For striped mullet, however, mercury burdens were not correlated with age, weight, or length.

A publication entitled "Your Guide to Eating Fish Caught in Florida," published by the Florida Department of Health (2007), provides consumption guidelines based upon mercury levels in freshwater and marine fish species. Fish that have more than 1.5 ppm of mercury in the edible flesh are considered unsafe for consumption. Those containing less than 0.5 ppm are considered safe for unlimited consumption. Consumption should be limited for fish with concentrations from 0.5 to 1.5 ppm. Using the most conservative consumption guidelines, those for women of childbearing age and young children, the guidelines that correspond to the results of this study, by sampling site and fish species, are available online: (*http://fisc.er.usgs.gov/maps/fishconsumptionguidelinesmercurylevels.html*).

All of the striped mullet samples that were collected (n = 67) from all sites fell into the category of unlimited consumption. Although the sample size was small (n = 3), all spotted seatrout from Oyster Bay (fig. 1) fell into the category of unlimited consumption; 93 percent of spotted seatrout from the lower Aucilla River (n = 15) also fell into the unlimited consumption category (table 12). No samples of spotted seatrout fell into the category of no consumption. For largemouth bass, 20 percent of those collected from Otter Lake (n = 20) and Lake Renfroe (n = 10) fell into the category of no consumption, but the remaining 80 percent were categorized as limited consumption (table 13). All largemouth bass from East River Pool (n = 18) were categorized as limited consumption; 50 percent of largemouth bass from the Upper Wakulla River (n = 12) were categorized as limited consumption and 50% as unlimited consumption (table 13). In addition, 90 percent of largemouth bass from Deer Point Lake (n = 20) were categorized as limited consumption, but 90 percent of largemouth bass from Martin Bayou (n = 20) were categorized as unlimited consumption (table 12). No samples of sunfish (n = 130) fell into the category of no consumption; however, 100 percent of sunfish (n = 10) collected from Lake Renfroe fell into the category of limited consumption (table 14). All of the sunfish samples from Martin Bayou (n = 20) and the Upper Wakulla River (n = 20) and 95 percent of those from East River Pool (n = 20) fell into the unlimited consumption category (table 14).

For spotted seatrout from St. Marks NWR (n = 31), 81 percent fell into the category of unlimited consumption, but only 40 percent of those from St. Andrew Bay (n = 10) fell into the same category. Half of the largemouth bass collected from St. Andrew Bay (n = 40) fell into the category of unlimited consumption, but only 15 percent from St. Marks NWR (n = 80) fell into this category (table 13).

Discussion

Mercury may be expelled into the environment through natural or anthropogenic sources and may be dispersed locally via an industrial effluent discharge or geographically through atmospheric deposition due to waste incineration or fossil fuel combustion. A survey that examined sediment contamination at the St. Marks NWR revealed that, although mercury contamination of sediments was not found on the refuge, it was found at five nearby non-refuge sites (Hemming and others, 2002). Urban stormwater runoff, industrial point-source discharges, historic oil spillage, recreational boats, and marina repair operations may be contributing to increased levels of mercury found in sediments of St. Andrew Bay (Brim, 1998). It is possible that mercury deposition in this region has resulted in increasing concentration of mercury in species of freshwater predatory fishes.

Mercury concentration levels found in musculature from largemouth bass and sunfish at the St. Marks NWR were significantly higher than those found in the same species of fish located near the non-refuge, urbanized St. Andrew Bay area (fig. 4). Although mercury concentrations found in musculature samples from spotted seatrout and striped mullet at St. Andrew Bay were significantly higher than those found in the same species of fish located at the St. Marks NWR, the spotted seatrout were collected from only one site at St. Andrew Bay, and the sample size (n=10) was relatively small. Collecting an adequate number of spotted seatrout within the legal slot limit at the bay was not possible. The sample of spotted seatrout was collected within West and North bays of St. Andrew Bay. West Bay receives thermal effluent from the Gulf Power Plant cooling system and municipal wastewater effluent from the City of Panama City Beach as well as moderate barge traffic through the Gulf Intracoastal Waterway. North Bay contains adjacent industrial facilities, including light industries, an international airport, and boat repair and manufacturing yards (Brim, 1998). Possibly because the estuary of the St. Marks NWR has less of these anthropogenic activities, lower levels of mercury were detected in musculature of spotted seatrout and striped mullet. Although statistically different, concentrations of mercury in striped mullet from St. Andrew Bay and St. Marks NWR were low relative to the other three species tested.

GSI, the ratio of gonad weight to body weight, and HSI, the ratio of liver weight to body weight, are commonly used endpoints in whole animal toxicity studies. Although GSI and HSI are not specific to a particular toxicant mechanism, they are good predictors of reproductive success and contaminant stress (Di Giulio and Tillitt, 1999; Slooff and others, 1983). This study showed positive correlations between mercury burden and GSI in male and female striped mullet. It also showed higher mean GSI values in estuarine fish from St. Andrew Bay, where mercury levels tended to be higher in these species (striped mullet and spotted seatrout). There was no correlative pattern between mercury burden and HSI in any of the species examined. Factors such as species' dietary and reproductive differences, the possible presence of additional contaminants and their synergistic interactions, as well as abiotic factors, such as dissolved oxygen levels, water hardness, salinity and temperature, may explain inconsistencies among these endpoints and mercury concentrations.

Numerous studies monitoring mercury levels in various species of fishes have been performed on a local level within Florida as well as on a national scale. Spotted seatrout collected from the following areas within the state of Florida displayed the following mean mercury concentrations: Apalachicola Bay (0.33 ppm), Charlotte Harbor (0.42 ppm), Florida Everglades (0.43 ppm), Choctawhatchee Bay (0.40 ppm), Indian River Lagoon (0.47 ppm), northeast Florida (0.16 ppm), and Tampa Bay (0.4 ppm) (Adams and others, 2003). Striped mullet collected from the following areas within the state of Florida displayed mean mercury concentrations: Charlotte Harbor (0.06 ppm), Choctawhatchee Bay (0.12) ppm, Indian River Lagoon (0.06 ppm), Florida Keys/Florida Bay (0.02 ppm), and Tampa Bay (0.08 ppm) (Adams and others, 2003).

Several species of fish, including spotted seatrout, crevalle jack (*Caranx hippos*), ladyfish (*Elops saurus*), bluefish (*Pomatomus saltatrix*), and gafftopsail catfish (*Bagre marinus*) that were sampled from Eastern Florida Bay, displayed mercury levels exceeding 0.5 ppm. The forage fish bay anchovy (*Anchoa mitchilli*), rainwater killifish (*Lucania parva*), and silver jenny (*Eucinostomus gula*) from the same area showed much lower mercury concentrations (0.165, 0.125, and 0.820 ug/g, respectively), suggesting that mercury is bioaccumulated as progression in the food chain occurs (Evans and Engel 1998).

The following mercury levels have been reported in other species of marine and estuarine fish: 0.78 ppm in bull sharks (*Carcharhinus leucas*) from the Indian River Lagoon, 0.39 ppm in snook (*Centropomus undecimalis*) from Tampa Bay, 0.68 ppm in gag (*Mycteroperca microlepis*) from Volusia County, 0.35 ppm in Spanish mackerel (*Scomberomorus maculatus*) from Apalachicola Bay, and 0.13 ppm in Gulf flounder (*Paralichthys albigutta*) from Apalachicola Bay (Adams et al. 2003). Mean total mercury levels in red drum (*Sciaenops ocellatus*) from the Florida Keys/Florida Bay area were 0.50 ppm (Adams and Onorato, 2005). The same study also showed that red drum from offshore waters adjacent to Tampa Bay contained mean mercury levels of 0.26 ppm.

Lange and others, (1994) examined mercury concentrations in largemouth bass, bluegill (*Lepomis macrochirus*), and redear sunfish (*L. microlophus*) from Lake Tohopekaliga, Florida. The mean mercury concentration for largemouth bass was 0.60 ppm, and the mean for the sunfish was 0.07 ppm. Largemouth bass in Florida also had mercury concentrations of 0.04 ppm from Lake Apopka, 0.15 ppm from Lake George, 0.56 ppm from Lake Istokpoga, 0.34 ppm from Lake Minneola, 0.17 ppm from Lake Okeechobee, 0.19 ppm from Lake Panasofkee, 0.49 ppm from Lake Placid, and 0.86 ppm from Lake Talquin, (Lange and others, 1993).

On a regional scale, mercury levels were shown by the Gulf States Marine Fisheries Commission (2002) to be relatively consistent within this report's study areas. Spotted seatrout from estuarine areas in Louisiana had mean mercury concentrations of 0.201 ppm, and spotted seatrout from Texas had mean mercury levels of 0.175 ppm (Piehler 2003, Sager 2004). Striped mullet in estuarine waters of Alabama and Louisiana displayed mercury levels below detectable limits (Alabama Department of Environmental Monitoring 2003, Piehler 2003).

Freshwater fish from Gulf Coast states also had mercury levels comparable to those found at our study sites. Mean tissue mercury concentrations of largemouth bass were 0.830 and 0.467 ppm from Texas and Louisiana, respectively (Texas Department of Health Seafood Safety Division 1995, Piehler 2003). Mean tissue mercury concentrations of sunfish from Texas and Louisiana were 0.39 ppm and 0.22 ppm, respectively (Texas Department of Health Seafood Safety Division 1995, Dupre and others, 1999).

Conclusions

(Correspond to Objectives/Hypotheses on p. 3-4)

1. Hypothesis rejected. Results support the hypothesis that mercury concentrations in fish musculature differ between St. Marks National Wildlife Refuge and St. Andrew Bay (non-national wildlife refuge area). Results also support the hypothesis that there are overall differences in mercury tissue concentrations among largemouth bass, sunfish, spotted seatrout, and striped mullet. The two freshwater species, largemouth bass and sunfish, sampled from the refuge had significantly higher mercury concentrations than those from the bay.

2. Hypothesis partially rejected. Mean gonadosomatic indices for male and female spotted seatrout from St. Andrew Bay were an order of magnitude higher than those for male and female spotted seatrout from St. Marks NWR, and male striped mullet gonadosomatic indices were at least one order of magnitude higher than those for male striped mullet from the refuge. Male and female largemouth bass and sunfish gonadosomatic indices did not differ markedly between areas. There were no consistent differences between areas in hepatosomatic indices for any of the species sampled.

3. Hypothesis partially rejected. Male and female striped mullet had positive correlations between mercury burden and gonadosomatic index, whereas male seatrout, male and female largemouth bass, and sunfish did not (female seatrout approached significance). Female sunfish had a negative correlation between mercury and gonadosomatic index. Mercury burden and hepatosomatic index were not correlated for any sex-species combination.

4. Hypothesis rejected, except for striped mullet. For three of the four species sampled, age, weight, and length were correlated with mercury concentration. In largemouth bass, sunfish, and spotted seatrout, age was the variable most highly correlated with mercury concentration. Weight and length were also correlated, but to a lesser degree.

5. The data collected during the present study are consistent with current advisories posted by the Florida Department of Health for water bodies within the study area, with the exception of Lake Renfroe. In this study, data for Lake Renfroe appear to be more consistent with the "once per month for all other individuals" advisory than the current advisory of "once per week for all other individuals." In addition, with regard to women of childbearing years and young children, data for Lake Renfroe are more consistent with the "do not eat" advisory than the current advisory of "once per month." Also, although the majority of largemouth bass were within the limits set forth by the Florida Department of Health, five individual fish that were collected in this study exceeded the 1.5 part per million limit advisory.

6. Conversely, although the Florida Department of Health recommends limiting the consumption of striped mullet caught in all coastal waters to two per week for women of childbearing age and young children, all samples of striped mullet collected in this study were below the 0.5 part per million limit advisory.

7. For all species but mullet, age, length, and weight were the most highly correlated characteristics with mercury burden. Although age is more expensive and difficult to determine, length and weight are readily determined, and these factors could be reasonable indicators of mercury exposure risk.

8. Periodic monitoring of mercury in St. Marks NWR and other areas in Florida will increase knowledge of mercury content and form in the various environmental compartments and aid in ensuring that fish consumption advisories and ecological risk assessments are based on the most current information.

9. Laboratory experiments in a controlled environment should be performed to validate observations and conclusions presented here on correlation of mercury concentrations with bioindicators, which were based on analyses of field data.

References Cited

Adams, D., McMichael, R., and Henderson, G., 2003, Mercury levels in marine and estuarine fishes of Florida 1989–2001: Florida Marine Research Institute Technical Report TR-9.

Adams, D., O'Conner, J.S., and Weisberg, S.B., 1998, Sediment quality of the NY/NJ Harbor System: EPA/902-R-98-001 US EPA, Region 2.

Adams, D., and Onorato, G, 2005, Mercury concentrations in red drum, *Scianenops ocellatus*, from estuarine and offshore waters of Florida: Marine Pollution Bulletin, v. 50, p. 291–300.

Alabama Department of Environmental Monitoring., 2003, ALIWQMAR CH8 (public health): Accessed November 2007 at: *http://www.adem.state.al.us/waterdivision/WQuality/305b/2006/2006%20AL%20IWQMAR%20Ch8%20(Public%20Health).pdf.*

Beyer, W.N., Spalding, M., and Morrison, D., 1997, Mercury concentrations in feathers of wading birds from Florida: Ambio, v. 26, p. 97–100.

Brim, M. S., 1998, Environmental contaminants evaluation of St. Andrew Bay, Florida: U.S. Fish and Wildlife Service Publication No. PCFO-EC-98-01 v. 1.

Brim, M.S., Bateman, D., Jarvis, R., and Carmody, G, 1992, Mercury and selenium concentrations in Largemouth Bass and other fishes of the Lower Suwannee National Wildlife Refuge: U.S. Fish and Wildlife Service Publication No. PCFO-EC-92-01.

Brim, M.S., Bateman, D., Jarvis, R., and Carmody, G, 1994, Mercury and selenium concentrations in fishes of the St. Vincent Wildlife Refuge: U.S. Fish and Wildlife Service Publication No. PCFO-EC-94-08.

Clapp, R., and Grandjean, P., 2002, Health effects of seafood contamination with methylmercury in the Faroes: Accessed December 2007 at: *http://www.masgc.org/Hg/abs-clapp.htm.*

Clarkson, T.W., 1994, The toxicology of mercury and its compounds, *In* Watras, C. J., and Huckabee, J.W., eds., Mercury Pollution: Integration and Synthesis: Boca Raton, Florida, CRC Press.

DiGiulio, R.T., and Tillitt, D.E., 1999, Reproductive and developmental effects of contaminants in oviparous vertebrates: SETAC Pellston Workshop on Reproductive and Developmental Effects of Contaminants in Oviparous Vertebrates; 13-18 July 1997, Fairmont Hot Springs, Anaconda, Montana, Published by the Society of Environmental Toxicology and Chemistry (SETAC), Pensacola, Florida, p. 297.

D'itri, P.A., and D'itri, F.M., 1977, Mercury Contamination: A Human Tragedy, John Wiley & Sons, U.S.A.

Dupre, T., Granier, T., Keife, S., Marino, R., O'Rourke, S., Partridge, C., Shultz, D., Mandhare, K., and Beck, J., 1999, Variation of mercury concentration in fish taken from Lake Boeuf, southeastern Louisiana: Microchemical Journal, v. 61, p. 156–164.

Evans, D., and Engel, D., 1998, Origin of elevated mercury concentrations from eastern Florida Bay: Accessed October 2007 at: *http://www.aoml.noaa.gov/ocd/sferpm/evans.html*.

Facemire, C.T., Augspurger, T., Bateman, D., Brim, M., Conzelman, P., Delchamps, S., Douglas, E., Inmon, L., Looney, K., Lopez, F., Masson, G., Morrison, D., Morse, N., and Robison, A., 1995, Impacts of mercury contamination in the southeastern United States: Water, Air, and Soil Pollution, v. 80, p. 923–926.

Facemire, G.F., and Chlebowski, L., 1991, Mercury contamination in a Wood Stork (*Mycteria americana*) from west-central Florida: U.S. Fish and Wildlife Service Publication No. VBFO-91-C03.

Florida Department of Environmental Protection, 2007, Plan for development of a statewide total maximum daily load for mercury (mercury TMDL): Bureau of Laboratories Division of Water Resource Management Division of Air Resource Management: Accessed November 2007 at: *http://www.dep.state.fl.us/Water/tmdl/docs/tmdls/merc-tmdl-plan-draft.pdf*.

Florida Department of Health, 2007, Your guide to eating fish caught in Florida: Accessed December 2007 at: *http://www.doh.state.fl.us/environment/community/fishconsumptionadvisories/fish_eating_guide.ng.pdf*

Goyer, R.A., and Clarkson, T.W., 2001, Toxic effects of metals, *in* Klassen, C.D., ed., Casarett and Doull's Toxicology: the Basic Science of Poisons, McGraw-Hill, New York, New York, p. 811–867.

Gross, T.S., Arnold, B. S., Sepulveda, M.S., and McDonald, K., 2003, Endocrine disrupting chemicals and endocrine active agents, *in* Hoffman, D. F., Rattner, B. A., Burton, G. A. Jr., and Cairns, J. Jr., eds., Handbook of Ecotoxicology, Lewis Publishers, Boca Raton, Florida, p. 1033–1098.

Gulf States Marine Fisheries Commission, 2002, Mercury forum speaker abstracts: Accessed November 2007 at: *http://www.masgc.org/Hg/abstracts.htm*.

Heinz, G.H., 1979, Eggshell thickness in mallards fed methylmercury: Bulletin of Environmental Contamination and Toxicology, v. 25, p. 498–502.

Hemming, J.M., Brim, M., and Jarvis, R., 2002, Sediment contamination survey on St. Marks National Wildlife Refuge: U.S. Fish and Wildlife Service Publication No. PCFO-EC 02-02.

Lange, T., Royals, H., and Connor, L., 1993, Influence of water chemistry on mercury concentration in Largemouth Bass from Florida lakes: Transactions of the American Fisheries Society, v. 122, p. 74–84.

Lange, T., Royals, H., and Connor, L., 1994, Mercury accumulation in largemouth bass (*Micropterus salmoides*) in a Florida lake: Archives of Environmental Contamination and Toxicology, v. 27, p. 446–471.

Nielson, L.A., and Johnson, D.L., eds., 1983, Fisheries Techniques, Southern Printing Company, Inc., Blacksburg, Virginia.

Piehler, C., 2003, Annual mercury report: Louisiana Department of Environmental Quality: Accessed October 2007 at: *http://www.deq.state.la.us/portal/Portals/0/surveillance/Hg/2003-Hg-Report.pdf.*

Rider, S.J., and Adams, D.H., 2000, Mercury concentrations in spotted seatrout (*Cynoscion nebulosus*) from northwest Florida: Gulf of Mexico Science, v. 18, p. 97–103.

Royals, H., and Lange, T., 1990, Mercury in Florida fish and wildlife: Wildlife, v. 44, p. 3–6.

Sager, D.R., 2004, Mercury in tissues of selected estuarine fishes from minimally impacted bays of coastal Texas: Bulletin of Environmental Contamination and Toxicology, v. 72, p. 149–156.

SAS Institute Inc., SAS 9.1.3 Help and Documentation, Cary, NC: SAS Institute Inc., 2000-2004.

Scherer, E., 1975, Avoidance of fenitrothion by goldfish (*Carassius auratus*): Bulletin of Environmental Contamination and Toxicology, v. 13, p. 492–496.

Scheuhammer, A.M., 1991, Methylmercury exposure and effects in piscivorous birds: Environmental Pollution, v. 71 p. 329–376.

Slooff, V., VanKreijl C.F., and Baars, A.J., 1983, Relative liver weights and xenobiotic-metabolizing enzymes of fish from polluted surface waters in the Netherlands: Aquatic Toxicology, v. 4, p. 1-14.

Stickney, R.R., Windom, H.L., White, D.B., and Taylor, F.E., 1975, Heavy metal concentrations in selected Georgia estuarine organisms and comparative food habit data, *in* Howell, F.G., Gentry, J.B., and Smith, M.H., eds., Mineral cycling in southeastern ecosystems: ERDA Symposium Series, Springfield, Virginia, available from National Technical Information Service CONF-740513, p. 256–267

Suter, G.W., 1993, Ecological Risk Assessment: Lewis Publ., Boca Raton, Florida, p. 501–502.

Texas Department of Health Seafood Safety Division, 1995, Assessment of risk for consumption taken from Caddo Lake: Accessed December 2007 at: *www.dshs.state.tx.us/seafood/PDF2/Risk%20Characterization/Caddo%20Lake%20RC%201995.pdf.*

U.S. Environmental Protection Agency, 1998, Test methods for evaluating solid waste, physical/chemical methods: SW-846, Update IVA ed., U.S. Government Printing Office, Washington, DC.

U.S. Environmental Protection Agency, 2000, Guidance for assessing chemical contaminant data for use in fish advisories: EPA 823/B-00-007. v. 1, Third Ed.

U.S. Environmental Protection Agency, 2001a, Emergency Planning and Community Right-to-Know Act, Section 313, Guidance for Reporting Toxic Chemicals: Mercury and Mercury Compounds Category: EPA-260-B-01-004.

U.S. Environmental Protection Agency, 2001b, Mercury update: Impact on fish advisories: EPA-823-F-01-011.

U.S. Environmental Protection Agency, 2006, EPA's roadmap for mercury: EPA-HQ-OPPT-2005-0013.

Vanderkooy, S., and Guindon-Tisdel, K., eds., 2003, A practical handbook for determining the ages of Gulf of Mexico Fishes: Gulf States Marine Fisheries Commission Publication No. 11, Ocean Springs, Mississippi.

Wood, P.B., White, J.H., Steffer, A., Wood, J.M., Facemire, C., and Percival, F., 1993, Mercury concentrations in tissues of Florida Bald eagles: Journal of Wildlife Management, v. 60, p. 178–185.

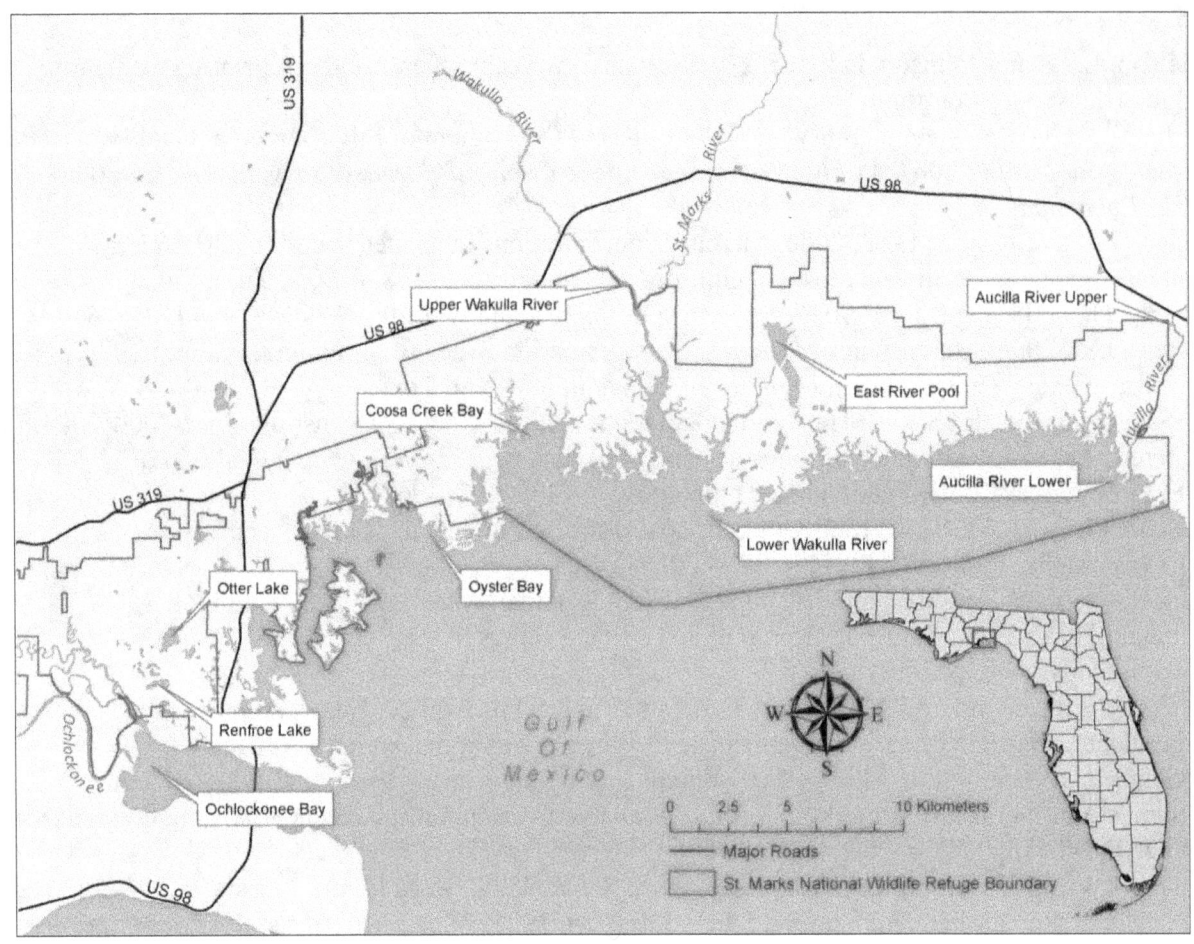

Figure 1. Fish sampling stations in the St. Marks National Wildlife Refuge study area.

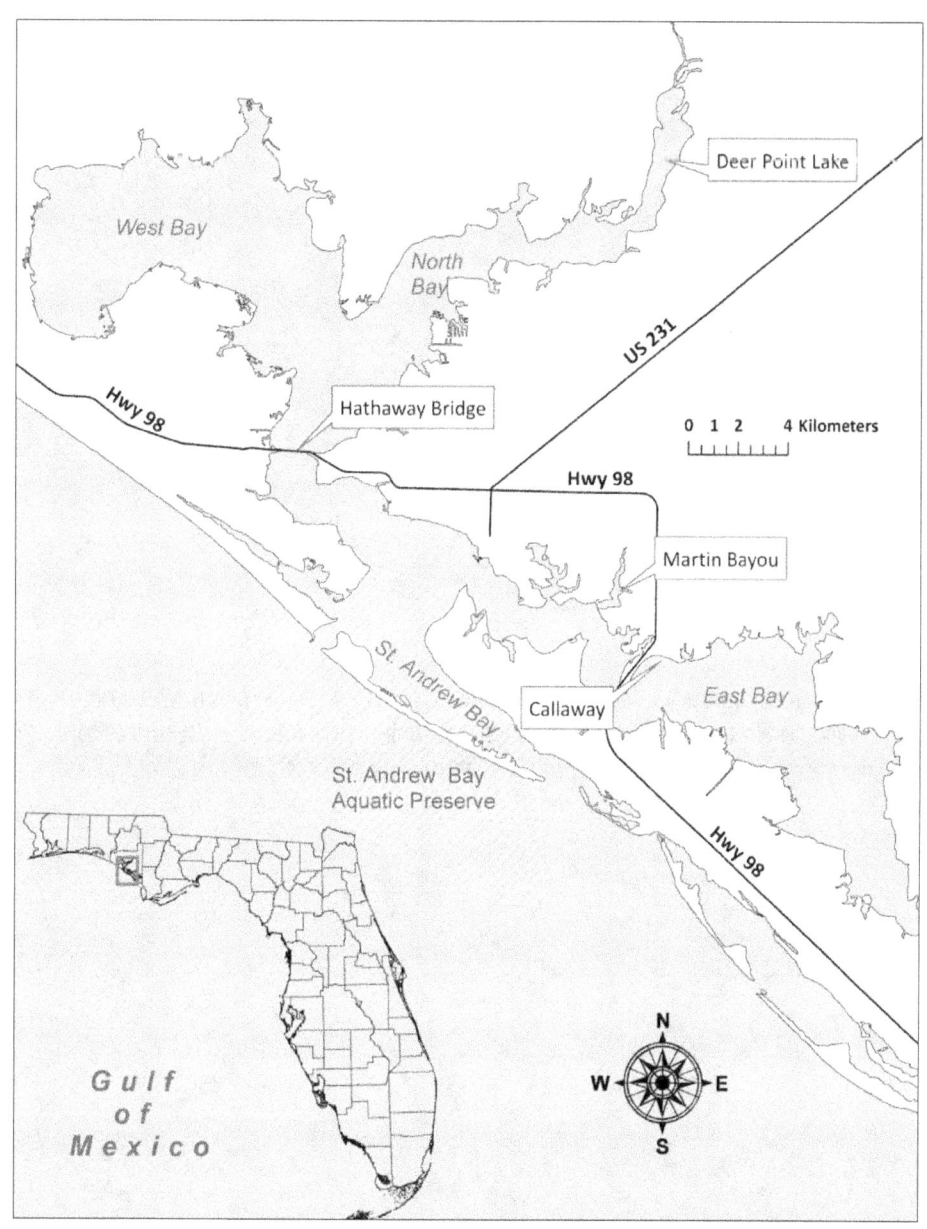

Figure 2. Fish sampling stations in the St. Andrew Bay study area.

15

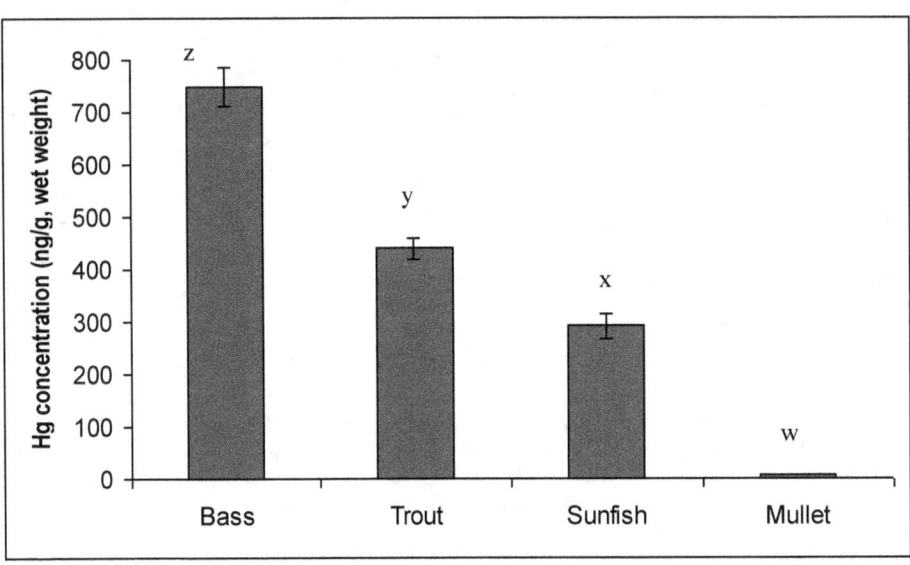

Figure 3.   Summary and comparisons of mercury tissue concentration (nanograms per gram, wet weight) in fish from St. Marks National Wildlife Refuge and St. Andrew Bay. Bars indicate mean ± SE and letters (z–w) indicate significant differences among adjusted means, with means adjusted for the effect of area (PROC MIXED, SAS 2006).

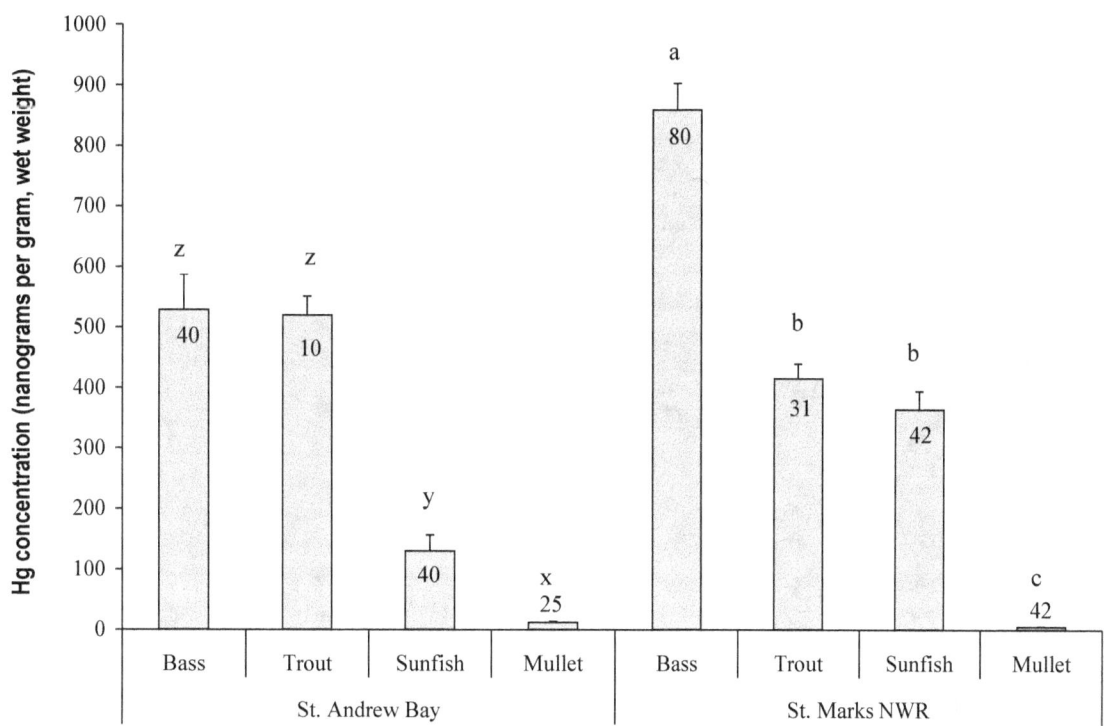

Figure 4. Summary and comparisons of mercury tissue concentrations (nanograms per gram, wet weight) for species from St. Marks National Wildlife Refuge and St. Andrew Bay. Bars indicate mean ± SE and numbers within/above bars indicate sample size. Letters (z–x, a–c) indicate significant differences between species within each site (PROC GLM, SAS 2006).

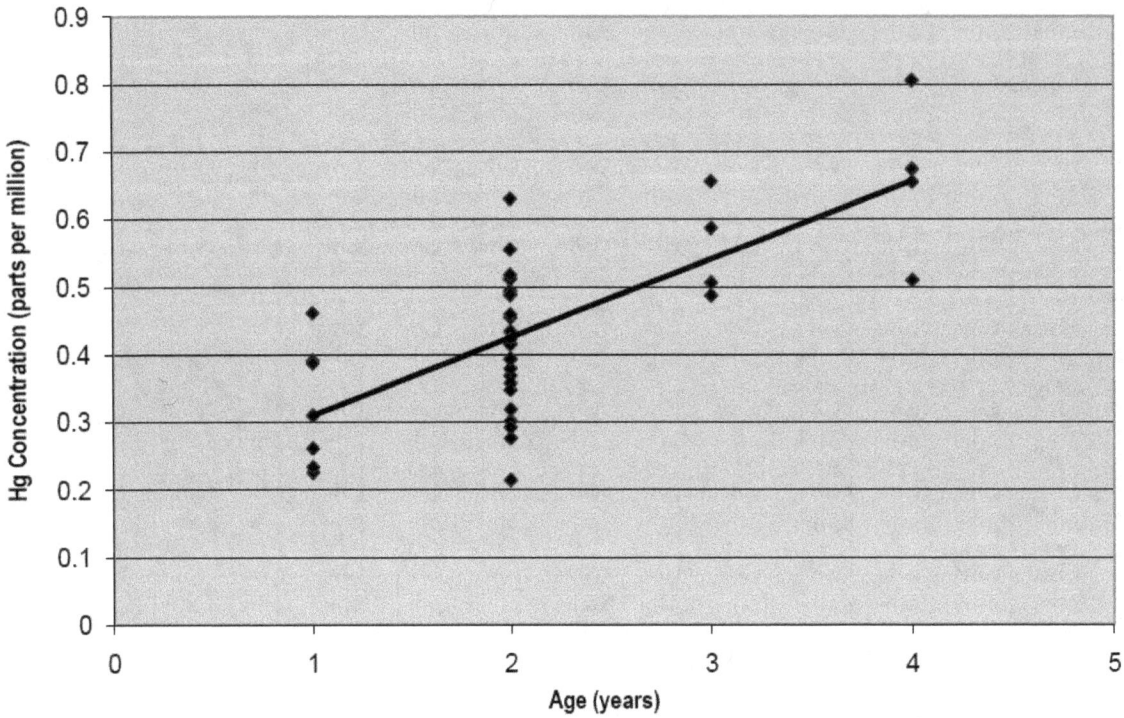

Figure 5. Examples of the distribution of mercury concentration in spotted seatrout with age for all seven study sites. The regression equation is $y = 0.1158x + 0.1938$; $r^2 = 0.5093$; p-value = 4.35 x 10-5.

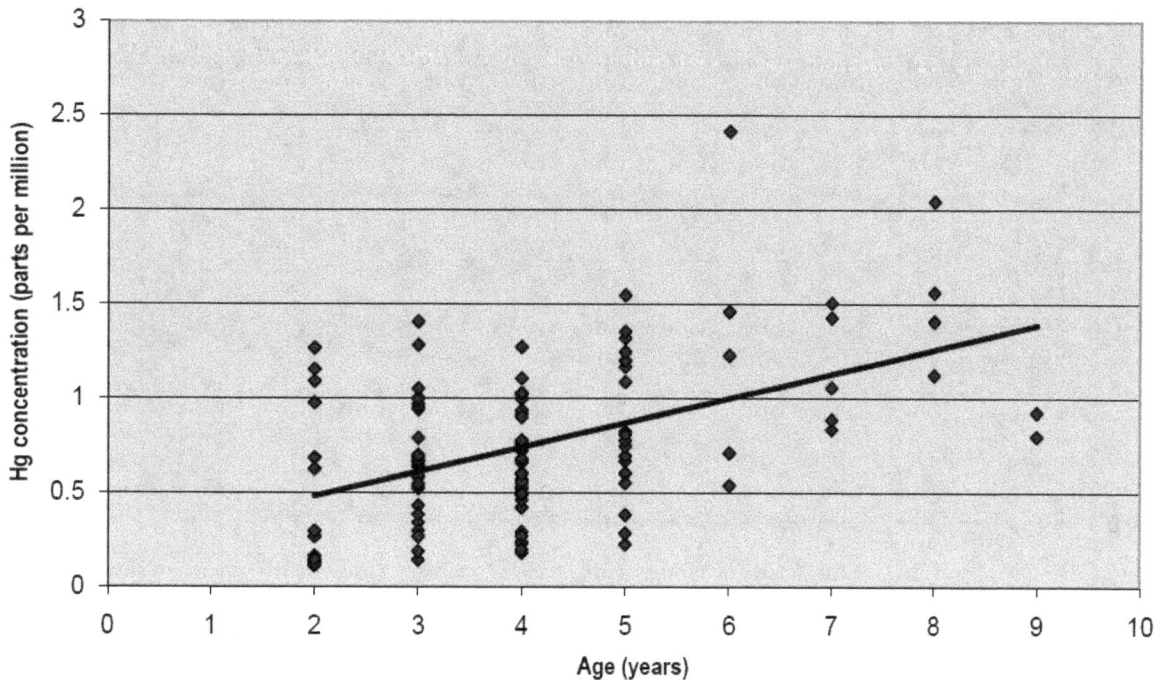

Figure 6. Examples of the distribution of mercury concentration in largemouth bass with age for all seven study sites. The regression equation is $y = 0.1293x + 0.2219$; $r^2 = 0.2361$; p-value = 0.0201.

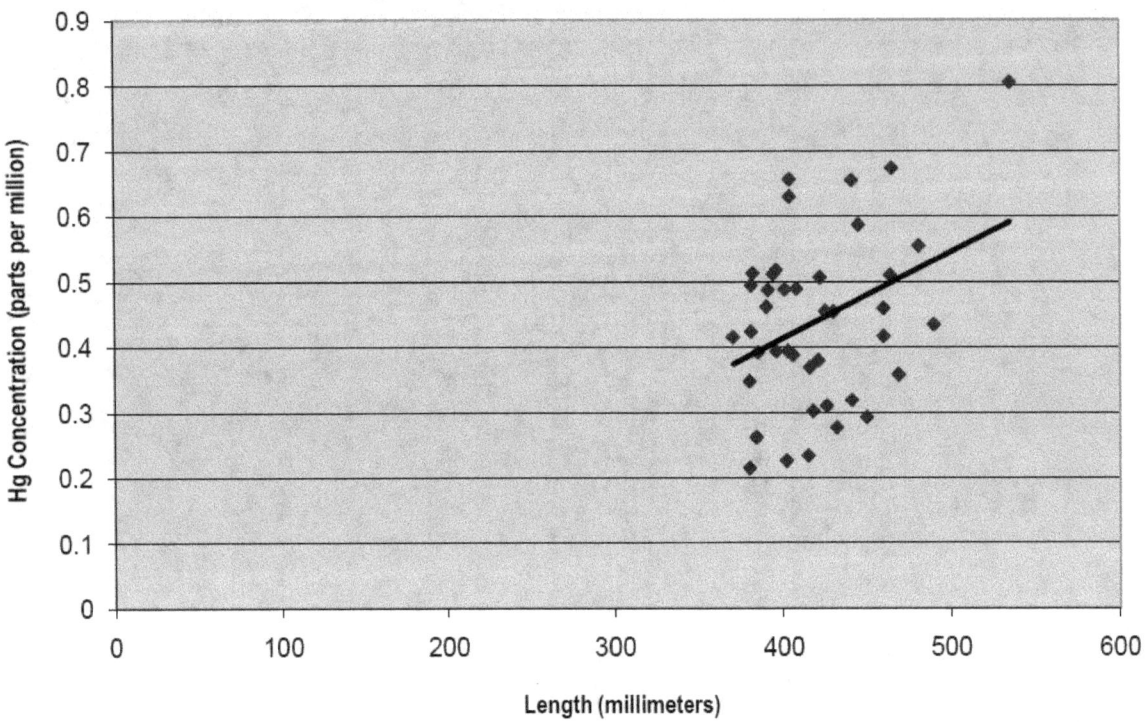

Figure 7. Examples of the distribution of mercury concentration in spotted seatrout with length for all seven study sites. The regression equation is $y = 0.0013x - 0.1154$; $r^2 = 0.1312$; p-value = 0.01994.

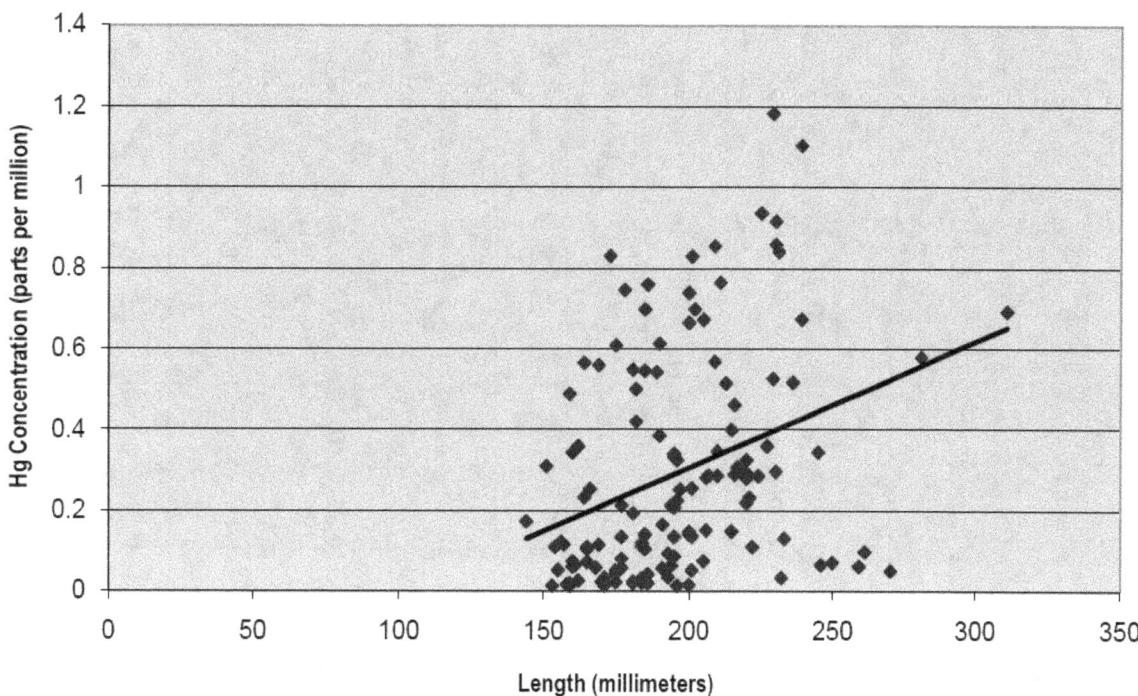

Figure 8. Examples of the distribution of mercury concentration in sunfish with length for all seven study sites. The regression equation is $y = 0.0031x - 0.3198$; $r^2 = 0.112$; p-value = 0.00024.

Table 1. Characteristics, mercury tissue concentrations (ng/g wet weight) and health parameters (hepatosomatic index [HSI], and gonadosomatic index [GSI]) of striped mullet from St. Marks National Wildlife Refuge and St. Andrew Bay, Florida, collected in July and September 2006. [Mean ± SE (N). Abbreviations: ARL, Aucilla River Lower, LWR, Lower Wakulla River, OCB=Ochlockonee Bay1

Area	Sex	Length (mm)	Mass (g)	Age (yr)	[Hg] (ng/g)	HSI	GSI
			St. Andrew				
	Female	412 ± 13.1 (10)	649 ± 55 (10)	3 ± 0.1 (8)	11.5 ± 2.4 (10)	1.3 ± 0.06 (10)	0.97 ± 0.19 (10)
	Male	379 ± 4.1 (15)	487 ± 18.2 (15)	3 ± 0.1 (13)	12.6 ± 1.81 (15)	1.5 ± 0.05 (15)	3.14 ± 0.845 (15)
			St. Marks				
ARL	Female	444 ± 4.5 (2)	1023 ± 33 (2)	3 ± 1 (2)	9.1 ± 0.8 (2)	1.5 ± 0.17 (2)	0.43 ± 0.031 (2)
	Male	272 ± 4 (18)	238 ± 9.5 (18)	2 ± 0.1 (18)	6.1 ± 0.4 (18)	1.4 ± 0.03 (18)	0.05 ± 0.008 (18)
LWR	Female	417 ± 9.1 (14)	927 ± 84.2 (14)	3 ± 0.2 (11)	3.2 ± 0.51 (14)	1.6 ± 0.07 (14)	0.69 ± 0.074 (14)
	Male	364 ± 8.8 (6)	530 ± 37.3 (6)	2 ± 0.3 (4)	3.5 ± 0.52 (6)	1.5 ± 0.08 (6)	0.23 ± 0.079 (6)
OCB	Female	399 ± 2.5 (2)	770 ± 20 (2)	3 ± 0 (2)	15.1 ± 0.38 (2)	1.7 ± 0.29 (2)	1.61 ± 0.462 (2)
	Male	No sample	No sample	No sample	No sample	No sample	No sample

Table 2. Characteristics, mercury tissue concentrations (ng/g wet weight) and health parameters (hepatosomatic index [HSI], and gonadosomatic index [GSI]) of spotted seatrout from St. Marks National Wildlife Refuge and St. Andrew Bay, Florida, collected during July and September 2006. [Mean ± SE (N). Abbreviations: HB, Hathaway Bridge, C, Callaway; ARL, Aucilla River Lower; GCB, Goose Creek Bay; LWR, Lower Wakulla River; OCB, Ochlockonee Bay; OYB, Oyster Bay]

Area[1]	Sex	Length (mm)	Mass (g)	Age (yr)	[Hg] (ng/g)	HSI	GSI
			St. Andrew				
HB	Female	414 ± 15.6 (7)	626 ± 75.4 (7)	3 ± 0.4 (7)	538.75 ± 35.02 (7)	1.0 ± 0.12 (7)	2.17 ± 0.44 (7)
	Male	386 ± 5.5 (2)	471 ± 21 (2)	3 ± 0.5 (2)	417.42 ± 69.81 (2)	0.47 ± 0.01 (2)	1.41 ± 0.03 (2)
C	Female	445 ± (1)	754 ± 0 (1)	3 ± 0 (1)	587.29 (1)	1.27 (1)	3.41 (1)
			St. Marks				
ARL	Female	431 ± 10.6 (11)	732 ± 58.3 (11)	2 ± 0.1 (11)	309.01 ± 23.05 (11)	1.07 ± 0.07 (11)	0.57 ± 0.02 (11)
	Male	401 ± 8.5 (4)	607 ± 43 (4)	2 ± 0.3 (4)	429.1 ± 26.6 (4)	1.09 ± 0.11 (4)	0.14 ± 0.02 (4)
GCB	Female	452 ± 27.7 (4)	922 ± 200.6 (4)	2 ± 0.9 (3)	467.64 ± 117.97 (4)	1.62 ± 0.06 (4)	0.55 ± 0.06 (4)
	Male	406 ± 2 (2)	620 ± 28 (2)	3 ± 0.5 (2)	572.69 ± 83.69 (2)	1.35 ± 0.04 (2)	0.19 ± 0.02 (2)
LWR	Female	385 ± 0 (1)	504 ± 0 (1)	1 ± 0 (1)	391.6 (1)	0.77 (1)	0.62 (1)
	Male	404 ± 0 (1)	634 ± 0 (1)	2 ± 0 (1)	630.15 (1)	1.25 (1)	0.19 (1)
OCB	Female	420 ± 20.8 (4)	627 ± 88.2 (4)	2 ± 0.3 (4)	473.02 ± 34.67 (4)	0.88 ± 0.07 (4)	0.56 ± 0.05 (4)
	Male	396 ± 0 (1)	538 ± 0 (1)	2 ± 0 (1)	517.46 (1)	1.1 ± (1)	0.13 (1)
OYB	Female	443 ± 17.5 (2)	832 ± 98 (2)	2 ± 0 (2)	456.95 ± 2.32 (2)	1.39 ± 0.03 (2)	0.66 ± 0.02 (2)
	Male	421 ± 0 (1)	606 ± 0 (1)	2 ± 0 (1)	379.4 (1)	0.76 (1)	0.13 (1)

Table 3. Characteristics, mercury tissue concentrations (ng/g wet weight) and health parameters (hepatosomatic index [HSI], and gonadosomatic index [GSI]) of largemouth bass from St. Marks National Wildlife Refuge and St. Andrew Bay, Florida, collected during July and September 2006. [Mean ± SE (N). Abbreviations: DPL, Deer Point Lake; MB, Martin Bayou; ARU, Aucilla River Upper; UWR, Upper Wakulla River; ERP, East River Pool; LR, Lake Renfroe; OL, Otter Lake]

Area[1]	Sex	Length (mm)	Mass (g)	Age (yr)	[Hg] (ng/g)	HSI	GSI
			St. Andrew				
DPL	Female	376.91 ± 18.16 (11)	744.55 ± 108.93 (11)	3.73 ± 0.49 (11)	610.63 ± 56.75 (11)	0.88 ± 0.06 (11)	0.32 ± 0.03 (11)
	Male	346.33 ± 8.35 (9)	554.89 ± 40.70 (9)	4.22 ± 0.32 (9)	1042.92 ± 92.76 (9)	0.79 ± 0.06 (9)	0.04 ± 0.004 (9)
MB	Female	384.36 ± 15.11 (11)	812.64 ± 105.52 (11)	3.36 ± 0.45 (11)	242.7 ± 46.10 (11)	0.73 ± 0.06 (11)	0.32 ± 0.03 (11)
	Male	358.33 ± 10.93 (9)	640.89 ± 72.43 (9)	3.22 ± 0.28 (9)	262.37 ± 50.5 (9)	0.86 ± 0.08 (9)	0.03 ± 0.003 (8)
			St. Marks				
ARU	Female	325.14 ± 12.95 (7)	442.29 ± 49.01 (7)	3.5 ± 0.22 (9)	602.54 ± 58.59 (9)	0.87 ± 0.07 (9)	0.91 ± 0.2 (9)
	Male	314.46 ± 4.61 (13)	408.0 ± 20.0 (13)	4.23 ± 0.32 (6)	625.19 ± 55.17 (7)	0.84 ± 0.05 (7)	1.09 ± 0.97 (7)
UWR	Female	369.63 ± 19.29 (8)	755.25 ± 128.83 (8)	4.0 ± 0.27 (13)	461.84 ± 56.21 (13)	1.02 ± 0.09 (13)	1.06 ± 0.35 (13)
	Male	327.5 ± 6.96 (4)	449.0 ± 32.30 (4)	4.25 ± 0.48 (8)	447.75 ± 76.83 (8)	0.82 ± 0.05 (8)	0.12 ± 0.02 (8)
ERP	Female	329.17 ± 16.79 (6)	442.0 ± 53.65 (6)	3.33 ± 0.33 (4)	762.37 ± 70.06 (4)	0.73 ± 0.07 (4)	0.34 ± 0.08 (4)
	Male	316.0 ± 6.13 (12)	405.67 ± 31.0 (12)	3.83 ± (6)	893.66 ± 51.05 (6)	0.8 ± 0.05 (6)	0.04 ± 0.002 (6)
LR	Female	341.57 ± 27.97 (7)	672.29 ± 215.08 (7)	4.57 ± 1.04 (12)	1345.66 ± 196.24 (12)	0.69 ± 0.05 (12)	0.26 ± 0.04 (12)
	Male	282.33 ± 6.89 (3)	294.0 ± 52.20 (3)	2.67 ± 0.33 (7)	975.07 ± 172.93 (7)	1.19 ± 0.38 (7)	0.03 ± 0.0007 (7)
OL	Female	384.1 ± 15.03 (10)	833.3 ± 102.91 (10)	5.8 ± 0.59 (10)	1190.22 ± 131.97 (10)	0.92 ± 0.05 (10)	0.29 ± 0.02 (10)
	Male	343.6 ± 12.29 (10)	612.8 ± 87.24 (10)	5.3 ± 0.65 (10)	1131.17 ± 92.31 (10)	0.86 ± 0.07 (9)	0.04 ± 0.005 (8)

Table 4. Characteristics, mercury tissue concentrations (ng/g wet weight) and health parameters (hepatosomatic index [HSI], and gonadosomatic index [GSI]) of sunfish from St. Marks National Wildlife Refuge and St. Andrew Bay, Florida, collected during July and September 2006. [Mean ± SE (N). Abbreviations: DPL, Deer Point Lake; MB, Martin Bayou; ARU, Aucilla River Upper; UWR, Upper Wakulla River; ERP, East River Pool; LR, Lake Renfroe; OL, Otter Lake]

Area[1]	Sex	Length (mm)	Mass (g)	Age (yr)	[Hg] (ng/g)	HSI	GSI
				St. Andrew			
DPL	Female	206.1 ± 11.56 (10)	174.2 ± 25.14 (10)	3.5 ± 0.70 (10)	192.92 ± 52.79 (10)	0.78 ± 0.04 (10)	1.16 ± 0.42 (10)
	Male	201.3 ± 7.73 (10)	169.6 ± 23.78 (10)	3.8 ± 0.55 (10)	270.51 ± 61.90 (10)	0.76 ± 0.05 (10)	0.25 ± 0.08 (8)
MB	Female	185.55 ± 7.28 (11)	133.09 ± 16.82 (11)	2.09 ± 0.37 (11)	27.26 ± 4.42 (11)	1.37 ± 0.11 (11)	3.31 ± 0.69 (11)
	Male	179.33 ± 10.84 (9)	124.22 ± 23.12 (9)	2.44 ± 0.29 (9)	29.09 ± 9.19 (9)	1.16 ± 0.12 (8)	0.34 ± 0.15 (7)
				St. Marks			
ARU	Female	202.33 ± 15.83 (9)	187.11 ± 63.02 (9)	3.0 ± 0.27 (8)	320.86±76.61 (9)	1.03 ± 0.08 (9)	2.74 ± 0.56 (9)
	Male	191.5 ± 7.02 (10)	138.6 ± 16.15 (10)	2.9 ± 0.28 (10)	205.98 ± 42.48 (10)	0.74 ± 0.09 (10)	0.33 ± 0.09 (10)
UWR	Female	224.8 ± 17.18 (5)	241.6 ± 55.32 (5)	3.8 ± 0.49 (5)	75.02 ± 17.25 (5)	1.17 ± 0.07 (5)	3.97 ± 0.80 (5)
	Male	183.87 ± 7.35 (15)	133.33 ± 13.10 (15)	3.0 ± 0.40 (15)	95.95 ± 18.01 (15)	0.93 ± 0.05 (15)	1.06 ± 0.46 (15)
ERP	Female	200.08 ± 5.71 (12)	170.33 ± 12.31 (12)	3.67 ± 0.45 (12)	287.76 ± 37.90 (12)	0.85 ± 0.03 (12)	2.60 ± 0.43 (12)
	Male	202.0 ± 9.29 (8)	184.0 ± 26.20 (8)	3.38 ± 0.38 (8)	238.55 ± 27.58 (8)	0.74 ± 0.04 (8)	0.75 ± 0.21 (6)
LR	Female	184.6 ± 8.80 (5)	130.4 ± 15.77 (5)	3.8 ± 0.37 (5)	654.08 ± 50.04 (5)	0.58 ± 0.08 (5)	0.43 ± 0.03 (5)
	Male	191.6 ± 4.91 (5)	153.6 ± 14.02 (5)	3.8 ± 0.20 (5)	662.78 ± 37.95 (5)	0.70 ± 0.02 (5)	0.12 ± 0.008 (5)
OL	Female	200.57 ± 7.14 (14)	159.86 ± 17.77(14)	3.79 ± (14)	709.76 ± 71.27 (14)	5.27 ± 4.59 (14)	0.60 ± 0.13 (14)
	Male	205.5 ± 11.64 (6)	184.33 ± 26.96 (6)	3.83 ± 0.40 (6)	598.55 ± 113.39 (6)	0.83 ± 0.09 (6)	0.07 ± 0.02 (6)

Table 5. Mercury concentrations in freshwater and estuarine fish species collected at St. Marks National Wildlife Refuge (SM) and St. Andrew Bay (AB).

[Mercury concentrations are listed in parts per million, mg/kg w.w.]

Site	Fish Species	n	Mean Hg Concentration	Range	Std dev
Aucilla River Upper, SM	Largemouth Bass	20	0.624	0.295-1.056	0.1808
	Sunfish	20	0.286	0.057-0.692	0.1963
East River Pool, SM	Largemouth Bass	18	0.853	0.559-1.167	0.1815
	Sunfish	20	0.268	0.105-0.517	0.1133
Otter Lake, SM	Largemouth Bass	20	1.161	0.548-2.043	0.3518
	Sunfish	20	0.676	0.292-1.182	0.2676
Lake Renfroe, SM	Largemouth Bass	10	1.234	0.667-2.413	0.4813
	Sunfish	10	0.658	0.546-0.830	0.0937
Wakulla River Upper, SM	Largemouth Bass	12	0.457	0.227-0.666	0.1502
	Sunfish	20	0.091	0.024-0.309	0.0631
Deerpoint Lake, AB	Largemouth Bass	20	0.805	0.263-1.458	0.3161
	Sunfish	20	0.232	0.052-0.665	0.1815
Martin Bayou, AB	Largemouth Bass	20	0.252	0.109-0.545	0.1485
	Sunfish	20	0.028	0.013-0.098	0.0208
Wakulla River Lower, SM	Spotted Sea Trout	2	0.511	0.390-0.630	0.1687
	Striped Mullet	20	0.003	0.001-0.007	0.0017
Oyster Bay, SM	Spotted Sea Trout	3	0.431	0.379-0.459	0.1619
	Striped Mullet	**0	**0	**0	
Goose Creek Bay, SM	Spotted Sea Trout	6	0.503	0.302-0.805	0.1978
	Striped Mullet	**0	**0	**0	
Aucilla River Lower, SM	Spotted Sea Trout	15	0.341	0.214-0.506	0.0883
	Striped Mullet	20	0.006	0.004-0.010	0.0019

Site	Fish Species	n	Mean Hg Concentration	Range	Std dev
"Ochlockonee Bay, SM"	Spotted Sea Trout	5	0.482	0.388-0.555	0.0711
	Striped Mullet	2	0.015	0.015-0.015	0.0005
"Hathaway Bridge, AB"	Spotted Sea Trout	9	0.512	0.348-0.674	0.1026
"Calloway, AB"	Spotted Sea Trout	1	0.587	0.587	.
St. Andrew Bay	Striped Mullet Composite Sample	25	0.012	0.003-0.027	0.0071
Largemouth bass					
St. Marks NWR		80	0.859	0.227-2.413	0.3931
St. Andrew Bay		40	0.528	0.007-0.393	0.3715
Sunfish					
St. Marks NWR		90	0.366	0.024-1.182	0.2833
St. Andrew Bay		40	0.13	0.013-0.665	0.164
Spotted seatrout					
St. Marks NWR		31	0.415	0.214-0.805	0.132
St. Andrew Bay		10	0.519	0.348-0.674	0.1
Striped mullet					
St. Marks NWR		42	0.005	0.000-0.015	0.0032
St. Andrew Bay		25	0.012	0.003-0.027	0.0071

*Hathaway Bridge and Calloway sites were combined as a composite sample. Each fish was individually analyzed for mercury concentration.

** 0 indicates that we were unable to collect samples of this species at this site.

"Samples were collected from July 25, 2006 to March 31, 2007. Mercury values were determined in 500mg-fish fillet sub-samples using a Direct Mercury Analyzer."

Table 6. Size characteristics, mercury concentrations, and health indicators for freshwater fish from St. Andrew Bay and St. Marks National Wildlife Refuge.
[Mean ± SE (N). Abbreviations: HSI, hepatosomatic index; GSI gonadosomatic index]

Descriptor	St. Andrew	St. Marks
Sunfish		
Female		
Length	195.3 ± 6.91 (21)	201.7 ± 4.67 (45)
Mass	152.7 ± 15.19 (21)	173.9 ± 15.35 (45)
Age	2.8 ± 0.41 (21)	3.6 ± 0.19 (44)
Hg[1]	106.15 ± 30.734 (21)	442.73 ± 44.45 (45)
HSI	1.09 ± 0.088 (21)	2.27 ± 1.424 (45)
GSI	2.29 ± 0.469 (21)	1.91 ± 0.256 (45)
Male		
Length	190.9 ± 6.86 (19)	192.7 ± 3.85 (44)
Mass	148.1 ± 17.02 (19)	153 ± 8.76 (44)
Age	3.2 ± 0.35 (19)	3.3 ± 0.18 (44)
Hg[1]	156.15 ± 42.819 (19)	279.83 ± 37.111 (44)
HSI	0.94 ± 0.074 (18)	0.81 ± 0.032 (44)
GSI	0.3 ± 0.081 (15)	0.59 ± 0.175 (42)
Largemouth bass		
Female		
Length	380.6 ± 11.56 (22)	353.7 ± 8.89 (38)
Mass	778.6 ± 74.37 (22)	653.4 ± 59.65 (38)
Age	3.5 ± 0.33 (22)	4.4 ± 0.3 (37)
Hg[1]	426.66 ± 53.706 (22)	889.7 ± 76.138 (38)
HSI	0.81 ± 0.045 (22)	0.86 ± 0.034 (38)
GSI	0.32 ± 0.024 (22)	0.57 ± 0.097 (38)
Male		
Length	352.3 ± 6.83 (18)	320.8 ± 4.4 (42)
Mass	597.9 ± 41.63 (18)	451.9 ± 26.6 (42)
Age	3.7 ± 0.24 (18)	4.3 ± 0.23 (42)
Hg[1]	652.64 ± 107.631 (18)	830.46 ± 48.104 (42)
HSI	0.83 ± 0.05 (18)	0.86 ± 0.039 (41)
GSI	0.04 ± 0.003 (17)	0.39 ± 0.315 (40)

[1]Mercury concentrations are listed in parts per billion, ng/g w.w.

Table 7. Size characteristics, mercury concentrations, and health indicators for estuarine fish from St. Andrew Bay and St. Marks National Wildlife Refuge.
[Mean ± SE (N) Abbreviations: HSI, hepatosomatic index; GSI gonadosomatic index]

Descriptor	St. Andrew	St. Marks
Striped mullet		
Female		
Length	412 ± 13.1 (10)	418 ± 7.5 (18)
Mass	649 ± 55 (10)	920 ± 66.7 (18)
Age	3 ± 0.1 (8)	3 ± 0.2 (15)
Hg[1]	11.5 ± 2.399 (10)	5.18 ± 1.036 (18)
HSI	1.28 ± 0.06 (10)	1.57 ± 0.065 (18)
GSI	0.97 ± 0.19 (10)	0.76 ± 0.102 (18)
Male		
Length	379 ± 4.1 (15)	295 ± 9 (24)
Mass	487 ± 18.2 (15)	311 ± 28.6 (24)
Age	3 ± 0.1 (13)	2 ± 0.1 (22)
Hg[1]	12.6 ± 1.807 (15)	5.44 ± 0.401 (24)
HSI	1.48 ± 0.049 (15)	1.41 ± 0.033 (24)
GSI	3.14 ± 0.845 (15)	0.09 ± 0.026 (24)
Spotted seatrout		
Female		
Length	417.8 ± 14.1 (8)	431.6 ± 8.33 (22)
Mass	642 ± 67.25 (8)	745.8 ± 51.5 (22)
Age	2.9 ± 0.35 (8)	1.8 ± 0.15 (21)
Hg[1]	544.8 ± 30.93 (8)	384.9 ± 28.37 (22)
HSI	1 ± 0.11 (8)	1.1 ± 0.07 (22)
GSI	2.3 ± 0.41 (8)	0.6 ± 0.02 (22)
Male		
Length	385.5 ± 5.5 (2)	403.9 ± 4.23 (9)
Mass	471 ± 21 (2)	605.1 ± 20.25 (9)
Age	2.5 ± 0.5 (2)	2.2 ± 0.15 (9)
Hg[1]	417.4 ± 69.81 (2)	487.6 ± 34.07 (9)
HSI	0.5 ± 0.01 (2)	1.1 ± 0.08 (9)
GSI	1.4 ± 0.03 (2)	0.2 ± 0.01 (9)

[1]Mercury concentrations are listed in parts per billion, ng/g w.w.

Table 8. Comparison of mercury concentrations with fish length, weight, age, hepatosomatic index (HSI), and gonadosomatic index (GSI), by sex and species of estuarine fish from St. Andrew Bay and St. Marks National Wildlife Refuge.

[r = Pearson correlation coefficient; p ≤ 0.003 considered significant (Bonferroni correction = 0.05/15) N − sample size; * indicates significant r value]

	Mullet female					
	Descriptor	Length	Weight	Age	Hg	HSI	GSI
Length	r		0.8208*	0.0373	0.1662	0.3656	0.3622
	p		<.0001	0.8657	0.3978	0.0557	0.0582
	N		28	23	28	28	28
Weight	r			-0.186	-0.1491	0.4289	0.158
	p			0.3954	0.4486	0.0227	0.422
	N			23	28	28	28
Age	r				0.1609	0.1398	-0.0423
	p				0.4631	0.5245	0.848
	N				23	23	23
Hg	r					-0.2028	0.5363*
	p					0.3005	0.0033
	N					28	28
HSI	r						0.2899
	p						0.1345
	N						28

	Mullet male					
	Descriptor	Length	Weight	Age	Hg	HSI	GSI
Length	r		0.9579*	0.5594*	0.3775	0.2569	0.4359
	p		<.0001	0.0005	0.0178	0.1143	0.0055
	N		39	35	39	39	39
Weight	r			0.4593	0.3091	0.219	0.3995
	p			0.0055	0.0555	0.1804	0.0117
	N			35	39	39	39
Age	r				0.3095	0.4269	0.1383
	p				0.0704	0.0105	0.428
	N				35	35	35
Hg	r					-0.0325	0.7369*
	p					0.844	<.0001
	N					39	39
HSI	r						-0.1737
	p						0.2903
	N						39

Table 8. Comparison of mercury concentrations with fish length, weight, age, hepatosomatic index (HSI), and gonadosomatic index (GSI), by sex and species of estuarine fish from St. Andrew Bay and St. Marks National Wildlife Refuge.—Continued

[r = Pearson correlation coefficient; p ≤ 0.008 considered significant (Bonferroni correction = 0.05/6) N = sample size; * indicates significant r value]

	Descriptor	Length	Weight	Age	Hg	HSI	GSI
Trout female							
Length	r		0.9597*	0.5749*	0.4758	0.3735	-0.1079
	p		<.0001	0.0011	0.0079	0.042	0.5701
	N		30	29	30	30	30
Weight	r			0.5484*	0.4837	0.4918	-0.1144
	p			0.0021	0.0068	0.0058	0.5469
	N			29	30	30	30
Age	r				0.74293*	0.269	0.4367
	p				0.0002	0.1582	0.0178
	N				29	29	29
Hg	r					0.2438	0.4915
	p					0.1942	0.0058
	N					30	30
HSI	r						0.0152
	p						0.9361
	N						30

	Descriptor	Length	Weight	Age	Hg	HSI	GSI
Trout male							
Length	r		0.7366	0.2385	0.2496	0.3747	-0.5175
	p		0.0097	0.4799	0.4591	0.2562	0.103
	N		11	11	11	11	11
Weight	r			0.1434	0.3692	0.5551	-0.6931
	p			0.674	0.2638	0.0763	0.018
	N			11	11	11	11
Age	r				0.4784	-0.1139	0.2688
	p				0.1366	0.7388	0.424
	N				11	11	11
Hg	r					0.4985	-0.2429
	p					0.1185	0.4716
	N					11	11
HSI	r						-0.7722
	p						0.0053
	N						11

Table 9. Comparison of mercury concentrations with fish length, weight, age, hepatosomatic index (HSI), and gonadosomatic index (GSI), by sex and species of freshwater fish from St. Andrew Bay and St. Marks National Wildlife Refuge.

[r = Pearson correlation coefficient; p ≤ 0.008 considered significant (Bonferroni correction = 0.05/6) N = sample size; * indicates significant r value]

	Descriptor	Length	Weight	Age	Hg	HSI	GSI
Bass female							
Length	r		0.9614*	0.4806*	0.2651	0.1381	0.0097
	p		<.0001	0.0001	0.0406	0.2925	0.9413
	N		60	59	60	60	60
Weight	r			0.5037*	0.3371	0.1894	0.02343
	p			<.0001	0.0084	0.147	0.859
	N			59	60	60	60
Age	r				0.4941*	0.1224	-0.0323
	p				<.0001	0.3555	0.8079
	N				59	59	59
Hg	r					0.0042	-0.1324
	p					0.9741	0.313
	N					60	60
HSI	r						0.2669
	p						0.0392
	N						60

	Descriptor	Length	Weight	Age	Hg	HSI	GSI
Bass male							
Length	r		0.9191*	0.3848*	0.1202	-0.2583	-0.0391
	p		<.0001	0.0024	0.3603	0.0482	0.7723
	N		60	60	60	59	57
Weight	r			0.4335*	0.155	-0.1103	-0.0321
	p			0.0005	0.2369	0.4053	0.8125
	N			60	60	59	57
Age	r				0.4745*	0.0362	0.0004
	p				0.0001	0.7852	0.9974
	N				60	59	57
Hg	r					-0.0276	-0.047
	p					0.8355	0.728
	N					59	57
HSI	r						0.0767
	p						0.5705
	N						57

Table 9. Comparison of mercury concentrations with fish length, weight, age, hepatosomatic index (HSI), and gonadosomatic index (GSI), by sex and species of freshwater fish from St. Andrew Bay and St. Marks National Wildlife Refuge.—Continued

[r = Pearson correlation coefficient; p ≤ 0.008 considered significant (Bonferroni correction = 0.05/6) N = sample size; * indicates significant r value]

	Descriptor	Length	Weight	Age	Hg	HSI	GSI
Sunfish female							
Length	r		0.9343*	0.7056*	0.3045	0.1181	0.0946
	p		<.0001	<.0001	0.0129	0.3449	0.4496
	N		66	65	66	66	66
Weight	r			0.6638*	0.2277	0.1282	0.1298
	p			<.0001	0.0659	0.3047	0.2989
	N			65	66	66	66
Age	r				0.5165*	0.1285	-0.1035
	p				<.0001	0.3075	0.4117
	N				65	65	65
Hg	r					-0.0362	-0.4131*
	p					0.7724	0.0006
	N					66	66
HSI	r						-0.0893
	p						0.4757
	N						66

	Descriptor	Length	Weight	Age	Hg	HSI	GSI
Sunfish male							
Length	r		0.9248*	0.7239*	0.3671*	-0.3033	-0.0905
	p		<.0001	<.0001	0.0031	0.0165	0.5029
	N		63	63	63	62	57
Weight	r			0.7700*	0.3703*	-0.2023	-0.065
	p			<.0001	0.0028	0.1148	0.6305
	N			63	63	62	57
Age	r				0.4177*	-0.06	-0.101
	p				0.0007	0.6427	0.4547
	N				63	62	57
Hg	r					-0.3307	-0.1916
	p					0.0087	0.1533
	N					62	57
HSI	r						0.0025
	p						0.9847
	N						57

Table 10. Comparison of mercury concentrations with length, weight, and age by species of freshwater fish from St. Andrew Bay and St. Marks National Wildlife Refuge..

[r = Pearson correlation coefficient; p ≤ 0.008 considered significant (Bonferroni correction = 0.05/6)
N = sample size; * indicates significant r value]

Bass					
	Statistic	Length	Weight	Age	Hg
Length	r		0.9563*	0.4150*	0.1791
	p		<.0001	<.0001	0.0503
	N		120	119	120
Weight	r			0.4440*	0.2387
	p			<.0001	0.0086
	N			119	120
Age	r				0.4859*
	p				<.0001
	N				119

Sunfish					
	Statistic	Length	Weight	Age	Hg
Length	r		0.9260*	0.7054*	0.3335*
	p		<.0001	<.0001	0.0001
	N		130	129	130
Weight	r			0.7011*	0.2769*
	p			<.0001	0.0014
	N			129	130
Age	r				0.4793*
	p				<.0001
	N				129

Table 11. Comparison of mercury concentrations with length, weight, and age by species of estuarine fish from St. Andrew Bay and St. Marks National Wildlife Refuge.

[r = Pearson correlation coefficient; p ≤ 0.008 considered significant (Bonferroni correction = 0.05/6)
N = sample size; * indicates significant r value]

Trout					
	Statistic	**Length**	**Weight**	**Age**	**Hg**
Length	r		0.9547*	0.4793*	0.3622
	p		<.0001	0.0018	0.0199
	N		41	40	41
Weight	r			0.4652*	0.3914
	p			0.0025	0.0114
	N			40	41
Age	r				0.7136*
	p				<.0001
	N				40

Mullet					
	Statistic	**Length**	**Weight**	**Age**	**Hg**
Length	r		0.8847*	0.5465*	0.1731
	p		<.0001	<.0001	0.1612
	N		67	58	67
Weight	r			0.3539*	-0.0237
	p			0.0064	0.849
	N			58	67
Age	r				0.2002
	p				0.1318
	N				58

Table 12. Percentage of spotted seatrout with consumption limits from sampling sites in St. Andrew Bay and St. Marks National Wildlife Refuge.

Site	Species	Percentage of unlimited consumption	Percentage of limited consumption	Percentage of no consumption	n
Lower Wakulla River	Spotted seatrout	50	50	0	2
Oyster Bay	Spotted seatrout	100	0	0	3
Goose Creek Bay	Spotted seatrout	67	33	0	6
Lower Aucilla River	Spotted seatrout	93	7	0	15
Ochlochonee Bay	Spotted seatrout	60	40	0	5
Callaway	Spotted seatrout	0	100	0	1
Hathaway Bridge	Spotted seatrout	44	56	0	9

Table 13. Percentage of largemouth bass with consumption limits from sampling sites in St. Andrew Bay and St. Marks National Wildlife Refuge.

Site	Species	Percentage of unlimited consumption	Percentage of limited consumption	Percentage of no consumption	n
Upper Aucilla River	Largemouth Bass	70	30	0	20
East River Pool	Largemouth Bass	0	100	0	18
Otter Lake	Largemouth Bass	0	80	20	20
Lake Renfroe	Largemouth Bass	0	80	20	10
Upper Wakulla River (CSM)	Largemouth Bass	50	50	0	12
Deer point Lake	Largemouth Bass	10	90	0	20
Martin Bayou	Largemouth Bass	90	10	0	20

Table 14. Percentage of sunfish with consumption limits from sampling sites in St. Andrew Bay and St. Marks National Wildlife Refuge.

Site	Species	Percentage of unlimited consumption	Percentage of limited consumption	Percentage of no consumption	n
Upper Aucilla River	Sunfish	80	20	0	20
East River Pool	Sunfish	95	5	0	20
Otter Lake	Sunfish	30	70	0	20
Lake Renfroe	Sunfish	0	100	0	10
Upper Wakulla River (CSM)	Sunfish	100	0	0	20
Deer point Lake	Sunfish	85	15	0	20
Martin Bayou	Sunfish	100	0	0	20